LET'S
see

The
American Flag

by Susan H. Gray

Content Adviser: Professor Sherry L. Field, Department of Social Science Education,

College of Education, The University of Georgia

Reading Adviser: Dr. Linda D. Labbo, Department of Reading Education,

College of Education, The University of Georgia

Compass Point Books

Minneapolis, Minnesota

Compass Point Books
3722 West 50th Street, #115
Minneapolis, MN 55410

Visit Compass Point Books on the Internet at *www.compasspointbooks.com* or e-mail your
request to *custserv@compasspointbooks.com*

Editors: E. Russell Primm and Emily J. Dolbear
Photo Researcher: Svetlana Zhurkina
Photo Selector: Catherine Neitge
Designer: Melissa Voda

Library of Congress Cataloging-in-Publication Data
Gray, Susan Heinrichs.
  The American flag / by Susan H. Gray.
    p. cm. — (Let's see library. Our nation)
  Includes index.
  ISBN 0-7565-0140-7 (lib. bdg.)
  1. Flags—United States—Juvenile literature. [1. Flags—United States.] I. Title. II. Series.
CR113 .G64 2001
929.9'2'0973—dc21   2001001582

Table of Contents

What Does the American Flag Look Like? 5

What Were America's Early Flags Like? 7

What Was Washington's Flag? 9

Who Made the First American Flag? 11

How Has the Flag Changed? 13

Who Wrote a Song about the Flag? 15

How Should We Treat the Flag? 17

Where Can You See the Flag? 19

What Does the Flag Mean to People? 21

Glossary 22

Did You Know? 22

Want to Know More? 23

Index 24

What Does the American Flag Look Like?

Every country has its own flag. The flag of the United States is red, white, and blue. It has thirteen stripes. The stripes are red and white. It also has fifty stars. The stars are white. They are in a blue rectangle in the top left corner of the flag.

The American flag did not always look the way it does today. Our country has had many different flags.

◄ *The United States flag has thirteen stripes and fifty stars.*

What Were America's Early Flags Like?

Many years ago, people came to America from England. They settled in places called **colonies**. The people were called colonists. The colonists had English flags. They lived in America, but they lived under English **rule**.

The king of England was not fair to the colonists. Soon, the colonists no longer wanted the king as their ruler. They made new flags. Some flags had snakes on them. Some flags had pine trees. The snakes and trees were **symbols** of their new land. They were signs of freedom.

◄ *American colonists dumped tea into Boston Harbor to protest unfair treatment by the king of England.*

What Was Washington's Flag?

The colonists began to fight with the British army. The colonists formed an army too. They started a **revolution**. They chose George Washington as their leader.

George Washington wanted a special flag for his army. This flag had the British flag in one corner. It also had red and white stripes. There were thirteen stripes. There was one stripe for each of the thirteen colonies. This flag is sometimes called the Grand Union flag.

The colonists won the Revolutionary War. Now they needed a new flag.

◄ *Some of the first American flags had rattlesnakes. Others had elements from the British flag.*

Who Made the First American Flag?

No one knows who made the first American flag. Some people say that Betsy Ross made it. Betsy Ross liked to sew. Sometimes, she sewed flags for the navy. George Washington may have asked Betsy Ross to make a flag for the new country.

The first American flag had thirteen stripes and thirteen stars. There was one star and one stripe for each of the colonies. The circle of stars was in a blue rectangle in the corner of the flag.

◄ *Betsy Ross may have made the first American flag.*

How Has the Flag Changed?

In time, America added two new states. These new states had to be added to the flag too. A new flag was made. It had fifteen stars and fifteen stripes.

Soon America added still more new states. If new stripes were added for all these states, the flag would be too big! Instead, a new star was added for each new state.

Now, our country has fifty states. The American flag has fifty stars—one for each state. The flag has only thirteen stripes. They stand for the first thirteen colonies.

◀ *When two states were added, the American flag had fifteen stars and fifteen stripes.*

Who Wrote a Song about the Flag?

Soon, America was at war with Britain again. The British army came to the United States in ships. The ships fired guns at a U.S. fort. A man named Francis Scott Key was in a boat near the fort. He watched the battle.

During the night, the guns stopped. Francis Scott Key was afraid that the Americans had lost the war. When the sun came up, he saw the fort. The American flag was still flying. The Americans had won! He was so happy that he wrote a poem. His poem was made into a song. The song is called "The Star-Spangled Banner."

◄ *After a battle with the British, Francis Scott Key was so happy to see the American flag was still flying that he wrote about it. His words are now the national anthem.*

How Should We Treat the Flag?

We should always treat our flag with **respect**. We should never fly the flag in bad weather. We should not let it fall on the ground. When the flag is flown at night, it should always have a light on it. The flag must also be folded a special way when it is taken off the flagpole.

◀ *We should respect the American flag. It represents the freedom of our country.*

Where Can You See the Flag?

You can see our flag in many places. It flies outside every post office in the country, for example. It flies outside city and state buildings too. There may be a flag outside your school. You may also have one in your classroom. Astronauts even put an American flag on the moon!

People also fly the flag at sports events. They stand and sing "The Star-Spangled Banner." Sometimes, you may see a flag that is only halfway up the flagpole. This means that an important person has died.

◄ *Astronauts put an American flag on the moon.*

What Does the Flag Mean to People?

The American flag is an important symbol. It helps us to remember all the people who built our country. It reminds us of all the people who fought for our freedom.

The American flag is a symbol of the United States. Every year, we honor the flag on June 14. This special day is called Flag Day. We also honor the flag when we say the "Pledge of **Allegiance**."

◀ *Some American flags are very big. These flags are on flagpoles on the side of a building.*

Glossary

allegiance—loyalty; support

colonies—areas settled by people from another country; these areas are governed by that country.

respect—a feeling of admiration

revolution—a violent uprising

rule—control by a person or government

symbols—objects that stand for something else

Did You Know?

• A flag flying upside down is a signal. It means, "Help me, I am in trouble!" This message is used only in emergencies.

• Flags are not thrown away. When they are worn out, they are burned.

• Francis Scott Key wrote his poem "The Star-Spangled Banner" on the back of an envelope. The music to the "Star-Spangled Banner" is from an old English song.

Want to Know More?

At the Library

Ansary, Mir Tamim. *Flag Day*. Chicago: Heinemann Library, 2001.
Quiri, Patricia Ryon. *The American Flag*. New York: Children's Press, 1998.
Ryan, Pam Munoz. *The Flag We Love*. Watertown, Mass.: Charlesbridge, 1996.
Wallner, Alexandra. *Betsy Ross*. New York: Holiday House, 1994.

On the Web

Flag of the United States of America
http://www.usflag.org/
For the history of Flag Day and pictures of the right way to fold the American flag

Flag Picture Gallery
http://www.ushistory.org/betsy/flagpics.html
For pictures of all the American flags—from the early flags with snakes and pine trees to the flag that flies today

Through the Mail

Fort McHenry National Monument
End of East Fort Avenue
Baltimore, MD 21230-5393
To learn about the fort where Francis Scott Key wrote "The Star-Spangled Banner" and about the Flag Day celebrations there

On the Road

National Museum of American History
Smithsonian Institution
Washington, DC 20560-0646
202/357-2700 or 202/357-1729
To see the real "Star-Spangled Banner," the flag that Francis Scott Key saw when he wrote his famous poem

Index

colonies, 7, 9, 11, 13
colonists, 7, 9
colors, 5
England, 7, 9, 15
Flag Day, 21
flying, 17, 19
folding, 17
Grand Union flag, 9
Key, Francis Scott, 15
lighting, 17
"Pledge of Allegiance," 21

revolution, 9
Revolutionary War, 9
Ross, Betsy, 11
"The Star-Spangled Banner," 15, 19
stars, 5, 11, 13
stripes, 5, 9, 11, 13
symbols, 7
Washington, George, 9, 11
weather, 17

About the Author
Susan H. Gray holds bachelor's and master's degrees in zoology from the University of Arkansas in Fayetteville. She has taught classes in general biology, human anatomy, and physiology. She has also worked as a freshwater biologist and scientific illustrator. In her twenty years as a writer, Susan H. Gray has covered many topics and written a variety of science books for children.